Art ligence

A Guide for the Perplexed

Simon Cross
Technology Ethics, Governance
and Regulation Policy Advisor

GROVE BOOKS LIMITED
RIDLEY HALL RD CAMBRIDGE CB3 9HU

Contents

First Impression July 2023
ISSN 1470-854X
ISBN 978 1 78827 325 1

1 Introduction

> Mitigating the risks of extinction from AI should be a global priority alongside other societal-scale risks such as pandemics and nuclear war.[1]

An innovation purportedly threatening the extinction of the human species; a new technology definitely disrupting our educational methods and approaches; a likely cause of mass redundancies. Yet also: a source of hope for medical diagnostics and therapeutics; the promise of increased efficiency in public transport (and of instantaneous and effective reactions in situations where things go wrong). And, whichever of these sets of predictions (or both) one focuses on, an astonishingly rapid pace of development; to give just one example, ChatGPT's latest iteration as GPT4 has in a short space of time 'learnt' to get a decent pass at mathematics examinations, and at least one Oxford academic sets his students essay questions along with an example of what ChatGPT could do with it. 'There's your first challenge: do better than that.' Yet of course the time might come, and might come quite soon, when the student, at least unassisted by technology, simply *cannot* 'do better than that.' Or so the story goes.

Artificial intelligence, or AI, has floated in the background of the human imagination for ages, being part of the fabric of science fiction and philosophical speculation. Related issues such as machine learning (ML) have been quietly improving in efficiency and increasing in pervasiveness, whether in the monitoring of processes (power supply, data transfer, exchange rate setting) or the reading of medical or industrial component scans. One purpose of this study is to think through the differing ambitions and approaches which might be encompassed under the label 'AI.' Some of these reflections, the more extreme ones, will point to important but controversial questions regarding machine consciousness and the nature of the human.

The headlines (whether hopeful or alarmist) regarding AI are not typically about these things, and mass redundancies are not premised upon fantasies (dreams or nightmares) about future machines that are conscious and can think, feel, or fall in love. In some ways the situation is a familiar one from industrial and post-industrial revolutions of previous times: developments in technology lead to at least high levels of disruption in employment as old skills become irrelevant or superseded, and new ones are needed. We may hope to learn from previous changes about how to manage the social challenges of these disruptions through the intervention of political authority and charitable effort, but we may also anticipate from previous technological changes and developments what some of the effects of these ones will be. They are likely to include greater levels of differentiation in accordance with skills and the perceived value of different occupations, and when associated with social factors which are independent of AI—an aging population requiring increasing levels of personal care, for example—might lead to a significant hollowing out of jobs in the middle ground between those requiring technical and analytical skills of a high order, on the one hand, and vital roles which require much less by way of educational attainment, on the other.

The goals of this study are, first, to lay out the central features of AI in non-technical language and, secondly, to indicate some of the key components of a theological framework for engaging with the wide range of questions and issues involved. The focus is in the main on the more abstract and theologically significant questions, rather than on policy questions in education or in healthcare. It will be obvious to anyone following developments in their field that if a week is a long time in politics, it is a very long time indeed in the world of AI! The questions dealt with here are not novel ones, though they might become more and more pressing as possibilities and ambitions for AI systems are extended in the coming months and years.

2

What is AI?

Whether through our exposure to Pinocchio, or Frankenstein's monster, or WALL-E, or Hal, or the Terminator, our ideas about the ways that artifice can be married with intelligence are mainly drawn from fiction and from the human capacity for imagination. While the so-called 'grand dream' of AI, a super-intelligent machine that is conscious and self-aware, remains within the province of the imagination, *Artificial General Intelligence (AGI)* is nonetheless a popular topic for discussion. The research project seeking that goal is still at a most formative stage and there are question marks about the long-term prospects of existing techniques for achieving so lofty an ambition. However, present day *Artificial Intelligence (AI),* the stuff that actually powers our smart devices and the services they run, is intriguing in its own right though the ingredients and claims made for them are more mundane.

AI Really Means Algorithms

How can one create a machine that acts 'intelligently'? Nick Polson and James Scott, in a very accessible primer on the underlying techniques that enable computers to act with what we call 'artificial intelligence,' say, simply enough, 'When you hear "AI," don't think of a droid. Think of an *algorithm*.'[2] An algorithm is a sequence of instructions to compute (calculate and / or act on inputs) in a specific order so as to calculate a final value as output. Algorithms can be of any length and they can be nested within one another so that discussion about 'the' Facebook, or YouTube, or Twitter algorithm should really be discussion of algorithms *plural*. Personalized social media feeds draw on a collection of perhaps hundreds of such algorithms to produce individualized content. The principle is straightforward but the resultant complexity means that, as the Facebook whistle-blower Francis Haugen testified to the US Congress in late 2021, only a small number of people inside Facebook actually understand how its own algorithms function, or their cumulative effects on users.[3] The impact of such highly complex algorithms, taken together with the lack of external accountability for their consequences, has raised a number of concerns.

So what is an algorithm? It is fundamentally a set of instructions of the kind "add '*a*' to '*b*' and divide by the sum of '*c*'," or "stop doing '*i*' if '*j*' happens" and so on. As the computer scientist Michael Wooldridge helpfully says, 'If we are to build intelligent machines, then their intelligence must ultimately reduce to simple, explicit instructions like these.'[4]

But the combination of faster and more powerful machines and the use of statistical inference, which is a type of reasoning that calculates probabilities for specific features in the data being analyzed, has opened up new and powerful opportunities. The mathematics for resolving this computational complexity is ultimately probabilistic; every AI algorithm computes the likelihood of its final sum or output being correct. To use a stock example, an algorithm can be trained to identify pictures of cats by showing it lots of examples of cat pictures (the training data) and then asking it to calculate the probability that a picture it has never seen before (the testing data) includes a cat. At its core, AI is thus about using logico-mathematical reasoning for pattern identification and pattern recognition, in order to make predictions.

From this basic method, three interesting and exciting possibilities emerge. First, there turn out to be a variety of computational structures and methods (machine learning, reinforcement learning, neural nets and so forth) by which to recognize and differentiate underlying patterns in the training data. The combination of increasingly complex physical processing structures (such as recursive neural nets which mimic the physiology of the human brain), together with ever cheaper storage and ever faster computational speed, has opened up new techniques for data analysis through novel mathematical techniques as well as increasing amounts of computational brute force.

Secondly, and this is a key feature of AI, in larger bodies of data this high-speed analysis using intricate and complex algorithms can be used to uncover underlying patterns that human analysis or intuition cannot discern. The more data, the more patterns there may be to discover and the more statistically robust those underlying relationships are likely to be. That is why it has, until recently, been fashionable to call data the 'new oil.'

A successful algorithm can only predict a pattern in data that does not yet even exist

It follows, thirdly, that successful algorithms can be used to predict the probability of a pattern or feature recurring in data that does not even yet exist, whether that is because such data has not been collected or because it is, in fact, a prediction about the future. Data is therefore the primary input that algorithms process for understanding the past and for predicting the future.

By iteratively (repeatedly) training, testing, and retraining, it is possible to tune an algorithm until the probability of, say, correctly identifying a cancerous tumour in a test image reaches a peak that matches or could even exceed that of the average human oncologist. Note, however, that this process depends on a number of factors including the quality and quantity of the training data (as wide as possible a variety, all of which is properly labelled) and recognizing that the AI's prediction is always probabilistic. It turns out that training an algorithm to find 100% of the cats in the training data actually *reduces* its overall effectiveness when it is presented with new data because the algorithm has identified patterns that are unique to the training data which is only a *partial* subset of the whole—a problem called 'overfitting.' Some of those perfectly matched patterns always break down or disappear as the set increases in size and diversity. An AI algorithm does not have to be told what pattern to look for; the whole point is to let the algorithm combine size of data and speed of computation to seek out patterns including those no human would or could find. Consequently, the leading edge of AI research is concerned primarily with discovering new combinations of structure and process for programming machines to infer *how to* detect patterns. Recent advances in image recognition disclose that the algorithm does not even have to detect patterns in exactly the same way we human beings do. The goal is only to create algorithmic tools that highlight patterns that correlate well in a given set of data.

Does the Algorithm Understand What it is Doing?

An algorithm is, then, a list of instructions, and while algorithms can be combined and interlinked to solve complex tasks, to date the final output of those instructions is always to solve a specific question or problem. That might be an AI that identifies cats, or predicts which houses in a municipality still have Victorian lead piping that threatens public health, or that predicts the maximum daytime temperature in central Paris seven days from now, or that predicts which video to suggest in order to keep a user viewing. Cumulatively the steps of inference might become highly complex, but the task the algorithm is tuned to perform is *narrow*. It was, for example, a significant landmark in AI when AlphaGo beat the world Go champion Lee Sedol in 2016. After all, a Go board has more possible combinations of black and white playing pieces than the number of atoms believed to exist in the universe. But AlphaGo has no idea what a cat is, or whether it is going to be cold on Thursday, or even what 'cold' means. And no one currently believes that Facebook's newsfeed algorithms understand the content they recommend.

The task the algorithm is tuned to perform is narrow

In the summer of 2022, a Google engineer provoked renewed debate about the possibility of AGI when he published transcripts of a conversation with a program he believed *had* become sentient.[5] The tool he was working on was a *language model for dialogue applications* (*LaMDA*). The question of whether the grand dream of self-conscious AGI is possible and how we might combine tools in a way that creates it—or indeed how we could ever really know whether and when AGI begins—raises questions that are the provenance of metaphysics, and debate continues amongst those who create both the physical and programming architectures of AI, as to whether *'strong'* AI is possible, let alone imminent. The terms *strong AI* and *AGI* are broadly interchangeable. Both terms are used to refer to self-conscious AI with agency recognizably similar our own. Plenty of computer scientists hold that only *weak* AI is possible and Google itself rejected any claims that its own LaMDA had become sentient.

But how could we ever tell whether or when an AI became an AGI, or strong AI? One of the most famous and popular evaluations of this question is the so-called Turing Test, first proposed by Alan Turing in 1950.[6] Turing regarded the question of whether a machine could think as too imprecise to answer usefully. A more objective test, he suggested, would be to let an interrogator pose the same questions to both a human and a computer for a fixed period of time after which the interrogator has to say which was the human and which the computer. Turing thought that by the end of the century we would all describe machines as thinking in the same sense that we do. This initial thought experiment has dominated discussion of AGI ever since and the recent controversy over Google's LaMDA suggests we may finally be entering the territory where a computer can carry on a human level conversation for five minutes in a way that convinces at least *some* people that it is conscious.

Does an AI that acts as if it is conscious therefore have to be conscious?

But does an AI that acts *as if* it is conscious therefore *have to be* conscious? The Turing Test is controversial because it deliberately side-steps what we might regard as the ordinary meaning of 'thinks' and concentrates only on the external output, the appearance. It is important to treat with caution some of the vocabulary we use when reflecting on these machine-human interactions. Some may think the word 'intelligence' is already a step too far; we placed the word 'recommend' in scare quotes above and could easily have done the same for 'understand.' Accusing an AI system of being biased can appear to ascribe personality to the algorithms, and threatens to resort to moral indignation instead of dispassionately seeking to understand where any problem might have arisen. (Of course, this might be traceable to human bias in the selection or labelling of, or otherwise be innate to, the training data.)[7]

A number of objections have been raised against the arguments of those who insist only a *truly* thinking machine could act in a way that closely resembles human thinking, probably the best known of which is by the philosopher John Searle. In his Chinese Room Argument, Searle imagines a native English speaker locked in a room where questions written in Chinese are slipped under the door.[8] The human agent does not, themself, understand Chinese writing or the meaning of any of the characters but there are books full of characters on the shelves and a step-by-step instruction manual on the bench telling them which characters to assemble and post back under the door for any and every combination that comes into the room. Thus, they are able to send the right strings of characters back out of the room even though they understand nothing about the incoming or outgoing character strings themselves. Searle insists the person in the room would pass Turing's test without actually understanding any of the questions or answers passing in or out of the room.

We shall pick up these disputed possibilities in chapter four—but for now it is important to note not only how but also *why* debates about the character and capacities of AI go beyond the debates about mathematics, science or engineering. It is because they raise profound and contended philosophical and theological questions about what exists and what can be known, and because they force us to consider the very essence and meaning of human being itself.

AI is a Catch-all, Generalized Name for Disparate Techniques

In summary then, AI is a catch-all term for a range of tools that take training data and then combine mathematical techniques in a specific set of steps—an algorithm—to identify patterns and relationships contained within that data. This pattern identification is tested, often repeatedly, in order to tune the algorithm to accomplish a single *narrow* specific task as effectively as possible.[9] Counterintuitively, the algorithm need not be told exactly *what* to look for, but it always needs to be told *how* to look. This freedom within constraint opens up exciting possibilities for making novel discoveries as data amasses. Success is defined statistically and good algorithms yield high probabilities for their predictions, but not certainties.

This raises one last point of clarification. The complexity of the whole process—the physical organization of the hardware involved, the mathematical and statistical techniques, and the method by which both are interlinked—are complex enough that giving a full account of the process can be difficult. This has given rise to the description of some algorithms or collections of algorithms as 'black boxes' inside which *no one* is able to peer. While it may be the case that only a few individuals have the requisite knowledge and understanding to know or name the full path from data input to algorithmic output, it is important to remember Michael Wooldridge's point that all black boxes are algorithms and that, no matter how many steps are involved, their outputs can in principle always be explained by tracing each instruction at every step.

3 Theological and Ethical Issues

The Distinctive Role of Language

To talk about AI at all involves language. In fact, language is one of the most powerful tools humanity has ever created. With language we can do more than just name an object. Language allows us to communicate *ideas* about objects, and even ideas about those ideas.

One crucial linguistic tool we have created is metaphor. If I refer to something in front of me as 'a plastic box containing more plastic, and copper, and silica and other items together with carefully controlled electromagnetism' I do not speak very elegantly! When I refer to that same arrangement as a 'neural network' I use metaphor as a tool. This particular metaphor draws on both the architecture of neurons in the human brain and an underlying model that links our own mind / brain structure to electronic computation. Metaphors are unavoidable for linking epistemology (how we know things) with ontology (what things there are to be known). Metaphors are, to coin a metaphor, the warp and weft of naming things truthfully where, as Rowan Williams says,

> To try to be truthful is to try and find a way of speaking that does maximal justice to the diversity and plurality of a situation, so that 'truthful' speech is inevitably committed to metaphor, in order to represent what we could call the overflow of significance that we confront.[10]

The idea that machines are doing the same kinds of tasks that humans do invites the use of familiar and *person*-al metaphors. Thus, it has become common to speak about AI 'learning,' 'deciding,' 'choosing' and so on. Furthermore, some metaphors are now commonly applied in the opposite direction, such that the human brain is now frequently described as a computer and the mind depicted as its software. According to popular writers like Yuval Noah Harari, neuroscience and psychology demonstrate how humans should be thought of as nothing more than 'hackable machines.'[11]

A metaphor is, then, a deliberately chosen linguistic means of transport. But in that case we need to choose both the right destination and the right vehicle for the journey. Does an AI algorithm 'learn' to 'recognize' cats in the fully-human sense of those words? Or does it only mimic some of the qualities we attach to such *self*-evident language? Should such descriptions of AI be taken at face value? We have already encountered the question of whether an apparent AGI could ever really have an internal mental life of the kind human minds experience. But if AI can only ever do so metaphorically, how might we decide where metaphor ends and the literal begins?

Such questions are familiar territory for Christian theology which has long wrestled with both the theory and practise of metaphor and analogy for linking what is familiar and human-like about God, whilst also respecting and preserving the absolute holiness (literally 'the *other*ness') of the divine. Janet Soskice, in her seminal book *Metaphor and Religious Language*, makes some crucial points about how metaphor works.[12] First, a valid metaphor is only so because it connects what is unfamiliar or new with what is already known on the basis of a single, *true*, underlying similarity. Secondly, the metaphor works as a whole, not as individual words. If Amazon's Alexa, say, is described as 'learning about the world' then the metaphor is carried by the whole sentence and its full meaning depends upon three distinct factors: the sign; the sign maker; and the thing signified. (These are sometimes called the subject, the vehicle, and the tenor of the metaphor.) All of these connect the speaker's intended meaning with the audience's interpretation through a wider social, political, economic and philosophical context. A really good metaphor allows us to reach what Rowan Williams calls the edge of a word and then continue swimming in the right direction. But metaphorical direction is intuitive and necessarily uncertain and no metaphor, however popular, can be used simply to vouch for itself. It may be common currency to refer to the mind as software but that ubiquity does not of itself ensure the metaphor is valid; it is possible for a widespread and popular metaphor to mislead.

A valid metaphor connects what is unfamiliar with what is already known

This may all seem rather arcane; it matters because metaphors are such powerful tools. Their use is a risky business. Metaphors can collapse without us even noticing their demise. Dead metaphors, like the 'hands' of a clock, abound in English. They occur when, for example, we abandon the word 'like' and say simply that 'the brain is a (sort of) computer.' Metaphors can also be overstretched, *lacking* the true underlying connection they claim. The challenge for language around AI is very real here because metaphors like 'learning,' 'deciding,' believing,' 'recognizing' and so on depend on a metaphysical leap involving a model of other minds that the metaphor itself cannot validate. When we are told that AlphaGo taught itself to play Go, appeals to efficacy ('the program played, and won') sidestep the metaphysical questions but do not resolve them, as Turing well understood.

A further issue worth noting is the modifying effect we now know technology has on its users. Our technological metaphors can actually retool *us*. One example has been labelled 'automation complacency,' a propensity to put too much trust in technology. Tesla, for example, has experienced a number of crashes because drivers placed too much confidence in the car's autopilot. Experimenters have also shown that in a simulated fire people will follow a robot in the wrong direction, ignoring clearly marked exit signs telling them the correct direction of escape and even after they had already experienced the robot leading them in the wrong direction earlier, so-called 'automation bias.'[13] In an echo of the 2022 Google *LaMDA* controversy, one of the earliest experiments to create a language-based programme, ELIZA mirrored the role of a therapist in Rogerian therapy, identifying and repeating key words from the user's typed input to form new questions as its reply.[14] Despite its simplicity and very narrowly defined capability, Joseph Weizenbaum was both startled and disturbed by the way users, including his own secretary, began anthropomorphizing ELIZA and treating it as a human confidante.

When it comes to interpreting the nature of AI there is, then, a powerful and indispensable role for language and consideration is needed of the ways in which we use it as a tool to connect the familiar with the novel. There are also our own, human preferences, tendencies and behaviours to consider including now-recognized human biases and our propensity to anthropomorphize.

The Formative Role of Society Itself

There is also a modulating effect on our attitude to AI that stems from the wider society we create and inhabit. In Western society today there is a still popular origins myth that insists science, after dawning briefly in ancient Greece, was displaced by the superstitions of Christianity until the early modern period. In *The Territories of Science and Religion,* Peter Harrison describes how the pursuit of what we now call science was actually associated with developing qualities of personal character at least up until the Middle Ages. Harrison describes how the meaning of 'science' changed because of the advent of a new tool:

> It is more than a happy coincidence that the idea of an accumulation of knowledge outside of the minds of individual knowers emerged just after the appearance of the new technology of the printed page, which made such a conception of knowledge possible in practical terms.[15]

While the warfare myth between science and religion has now been discredited as an artifice or polemic, rather than as a historically accurate account, the Enlightenment notion that human progress and technological progress are intertwined still prevails in our culture. Furthermore, the threats posed by the climate and ecological crises have only increased our dependence on tomorrow's technologies and the tools of AI to save us from today's problems and perils. For some technologists, AI is the upcoming escape vehicle, literally, for a future humanity traversing the stars.[16]

Since the new tools of AI and the technologies of digital computing on which it depends are necessarily barely a century old, however, the entire debate and the preferential metaphors that have formed it can all be located within a frame of reference that has removed both theology and transcendence from the way we human beings perceive ourselves and the world around us.

In the context of AGI this is sometimes used just to side step the metaphysical question of what thinking involves, as Turing did, to bracket out the questions of consciousness and of the subject. But some discussions of AGI adopt the perspective that all observable behaviour can be explained without recourse to anything like an inner mind of a conscious subject. The result has been a dominant form of language use which drops the cautionary quotation marks, with AI univocally described simply as *learning* or *preferring* or *deciding* in a sense that is literally substitutable with human manifestations of these states. At the same time, any non-materialist explanation of human consciousness and any spiritual dimension of human being is rejected as defective. That human beings may be more than the physical is dismissed, after which it is but a short step to further conclude that an AI has genuine human-like capabilities on the basis of its external behaviour alone.

> **The tools and machines we have built have become indistinguishable from us**

The sense of historical progress is clear: once, we were superior in some sense to every tool or machine we created. But eventually the tools and machines showed us how we too are only machines, fashioned by the slow blunt tools of time and chance. Now, the tools and machines we have built have become indistinguishable from us. Soon they will overtake us. We will lose control of our own tools. Hopefully we might yet somehow create them in a way that saves us (not least from ourselves!). Or so the doomsayer argument goes.[17, 18]

Money as a Tool for Tools

There is a third strong motivation for using language about human beings and our machines non-metaphorically. Vested and powerful economic interests funding technology and AI in particular see much to gain either in power and political control or in monetary and economic control, by eliminating any *fundamental* distinction between humans and machines, not least because a version of me that can be replicated and scaled at almost zero marginal cost (but unlike me never needs to sleep, or eat, or take a holiday, or see a doctor), sounds really good, really *efficient*, really profitable—at least to someone.

Three conclusions follow for the debate about AI that will inform the rest of this book. First, very careful attention has to be paid to the way that language is being used to make and to justify claims, both in describing what current tools of AI are doing and when contemplating the possibility of AGI. Language is a powerful tool in its own right and the role(s) and risks of metaphors in popular depictions of AI are not always sufficiently recognized or critiqued. This scrutiny matters because of both the philosophical implications for human self-understanding and for AI's practical social, political and economic impacts as well.

Secondly, this commonplace understanding of what the term AI refers to depends on a culturally-tuned understanding of what it means to be a human being that must, itself, be framed in a broader social and historical context.

In light of these factors, Christian theology can and should offer a corrective to depictions of AI that reductively present the human mind as a machine, and that on the flip side, as it were, in turn over-attribute human qualities of mind to state-of-the-art AI techniques and programs. The risk, to paraphrase John the Baptist, is that we inadvertently become less in order that they—that is, our tools and our machines—might become more.

4

AI and Human Being

As we start interrogating the meaning of 'artificial intelligence' our attention unavoidably converges on a single central question: what it means to be human. Biblical anthropology asserts the dignity, value and purpose of human being in relationship, a way of being that is in relationship with fellow humans and with the created order and that is in relationship to God who is the ultimate source of all meaning, value and purpose. In contrast, much modern secular thinking envisages human being in exclusively physicalist and naturalist terms, both the world and human being having no inherent meaning or purpose. It is helpful to compare and contrast this biblical anthropology with the anthropology usually applied to AI in order to identify key differences as well as similarities between the two worldviews. These reflections might in fact lead us back from reflection on artificial intelligence to think more deeply on what it is to be human, made in the image of God.

Mind, Body and Soul

In whose image is AI being formed? Could God (or we?) breathe life into an object created from pre-existing material and formed to possess artificial intelligence? There are no obvious *a priori* grounds for denying the possibility and thus, however sceptical we may be of the possibility, no clear basis definitively to reject it.

Science has identified the principle of emergence in which complex behaviour can arise through the interaction of simple individual components. In an emergent phenomenon, the whole becomes more than the sum of its parts. But when and how is this possible? And is the appeal to emergence merely descriptive of *what* happens, or is it explanatory of *how* it happens? Science, properly conceived, is conducted on the basis of *methodological* naturalism, limiting the explanations it seeks and accepts to those typically framed in terms of physical and chemical processes. Methodological naturalism brackets out the question of spirit having any explanatory role, but the extent to which *being alive* and simply *being* are metaphysically separate and distinct steps remains both scientifically and philosophically opaque, as does therefore the possibility of a complete understanding of the human in scientific terms. Science properly understood cannot, in any event, be used to deny the possibility of a non-physical spirit without reaching beyond its own methodological boundaries. There is no settled scientific *explanation* for consciousness and no distinct or definitive line to separate animate life from non-life. This might be because no such demarcation exists. But it might also be because science is by its own proper method blind to some dimension(s) of being.

It was the divine will for the second person of the Trinity to be born and to live bodily among human beings as a fellow human being in order to reveal and to save. There could be no Christianity without the embodied and *human* Christ, Jesus. Embodiment should therefore be viewed as a key component for the *similarity* of divine identity with human being. The incarnation grounds the metaphor. AI systems necessarily rely on physical substrates but can be ported between them, raising speculative philosophical questions about identity which may encourage reflection upon human identity and its relation to the physical as well.

The theological conception of the human soul stems from the Hebrew word *nephesh* and the Greek word *psyche*. Despite the fact that methodological naturalism cannot experimentally prove—or *disprove*—the existence or nature of the soul, we may feel the weight of the questions of what creates and constitutes the 'me' that only 'I' can access directly, and what happens to that 'me' when I die. The *Catholic Encyclopaedia* defines the soul as

> ...the ultimate internal principle by which we think, feel, and will, and by which our bodies are animated...That our vital activities proceed from a principle capable of subsisting in itself, is the thesis of the substantiality of the soul: that this principle is not itself composite, extended, corporeal, or essentially and intrinsically dependent on the body, is the doctrine of spirituality.[19]

In ancient Greece the soul was a distinguishing feature of living beings, the seat of emotions and ideas and the virtues. The notion of soul is therefore a helpful, albeit disputed, concept for protecting ourselves from our own tendency to anthropomorphize objects and processes. In 2021, for example, Prem Natarajan of Amazon Science talked about

> ...what I like to think of as a new 'age of self' in artificial intelligence, an age in which AI systems such as Alexa become more self-aware and more self-learning, and in which they lend themselves to self-service by experienced developers and even end users.[20]

The use of a familiar and human name like Alexa as a trigger phrase tempts us to drop the quotation marks and treat Alexa as another person. And yet Alexa cannot have even a metaphorical or analogical soul because Alexa is a computer program shared across disparate servers, databases, and devices. Alexa cannot enter the age of self if there is no single coherent seat of identity as a constituted being. Alexa is not even a single unified algorithm. One of her algorithms can always tell you the time where you are, even doing so in universal time coordinates if you ask, but Alexa cannot *know* the time *her-self* in the same sense that *you* know time, any more than you can simultaneously 'know' the time in every time zone of the world. Alexa is, curiously, in this limited sense just slightly more as we may imagine God (less limited in location, say) than we are; but less like God as God chose to be revealed to us in Christ. Which may lead us to reflect on what it really means to be created in God's image and likeness.

Free Will, Character and Purpose

If an AI is always reducible to an algorithm, and if an algorithm is always reducible to a step-by-step set of actions, then could AI ever possess free will? In the case of narrow AI this is philosophically straightforward because no free agency is even being claimed. A lethal autonomous weapon like a military drone has no free will and, while the ethical issues are undoubtedly complicated, the autonomy of the drone's targeting system is always and only a function of the algorithmic program it is executing line of code by line of code. A drone circling a city is only metaphorically autonomous, independent of human agency but having no meaningful intentions of its own.

The autonomy of a drone is always a function of its algorithms

But maybe human free will is just an illusion and we, too, are ineluctably destined to act in whatever ways we do. As previously noted, there is a risk (tendency even?) to close the gap between us and our artificially intelligent tools by reducing the full dimensionality of human being and insisting that we are just computers on legs. But moral responsibility cannot easily be detached from the ability to choose otherwise. So, when an AI rejects a loan application based on postcode, or chooses a target for its next missile, or misidentifies a cancerous tumour as benign, or eliminates a candidate when screening their CV, and so on, who should be held responsible for any injustice? Can morally responsible AI create itself or does there need always to be a human either 'in the loop' or 'on the loop' to impart and accept final moral responsibility for the outcome of every algorithm?

Any disquiet about excluding humans from the responsibility loop helps, again, to signify the difference between artificial intelligence and human being. Expelling human oversight and final responsibility, shifting the moral blame onto the AI, as it were, shortcuts a biblical anthropology that situates human being firmly in a framework of appreciation of values, moral and aesthetic, and of choices and agency that are themselves a participation in the image of God. The questions that attend AGI are interesting and sometimes dramatic, but they are also entirely speculative at this stage, and there is no reason to think that AI systems share any of these features of human being. It is worth stressing again that there are still significant conceptual breakthroughs standing between the latest technological tools we are creating and anything close to the full dimensionality of human being and human agency.[21]

There may, though, be some room for theological reflection here on the role which humans find themselves in. Free or otherwise, few doubt the potentially destructive capacity of AI, and the possibilities of economic and social differentiation and division. Will humans be willing, will they be able, to take responsibility for what they unleash? And that thought may in turn reflect back onto our sense of the responsibility which Christians see God taking in the life and death of Jesus—which may lead at least to humility, and to our responsibility for that which God has entrusted to us—which may make us properly cautious. Our machines and AI systems lack the agency to be sensibly accused of pride, greed and sin. With humans it is not so; yet God both created us and chooses to bear responsibility for us.

Practical Theology and Artificial Intelligence

5

The underlying philosophical questions about AGI or digitally-mediated transhumanism of the kind Elon Musk hopes his Neuralink devices will eventually model, remain theoretical. Consequently, our primary focus should be on those theological and ethical concerns that are both present and increasingly urgent. Broadly this means focusing on issues of stewardship of these current forms of AI for the broader benefit of both society and the natural world.

Environmental Impacts of AI

Once again the language, the preferred names for the hidden but material aspects of AI, have great potential to mislead. The cloud to which we upload our holiday photos is not in fact virtual, immaterial or ethereal. It is, rather a globally-interconnected network of buildings, often the size of several football pitches, made from vast amounts of steel and concrete, and requiring vast amounts of electrical power both to energize rack after rack of processor and storage devices and to expel the unavoidable by-product of all that computational work—heat. Our smartphones may be wireless but as scholars like Kate Crawford have helped to show, they connect to a literal and physical worldwide web that depends on cables made from physical resources like copper and steel and plastic and silica, and stretch across vast oceans in order literally to encompass the globe.[22]

AI is a wonderful tool for improving some kinds of human endeavour. AI is now being used to design some its own components faster. AI is being used to discover new patterns in big data sets and to reveal both new opportunities and unrecognized needs in the world around us.[23] But e-waste which, according to the UN, now amounts to more than fifty million tonnes per year, is a significant and growing challenge for society not only as a quantitative problem but also because some of the source materials used to fabricate the physical components needed by these smart new AI tools are highly toxic.[24] Rare earth minerals that are not recycled place growing pressure on remaining supplies. This is a complex and important ethical dimension of AI in part because the UK is one of the largest producers of e-waste in the world, and in part because impoverished countries of the majority world supply a hidden workforce, including child labour, first to extract the raw minerals and then to receive the discarded produce of Western consumers.

Some of the specific tools of AI are becoming worryingly energy-intensive in their own right. The process of training, testing and tuning *large language models* (LLMs) in particular, like the Google LaMDA mentioned earlier, is now exhibiting a power law whereby the amount of energy required (measured in units of electricity, processor capacity, training data and time) is ever-increasing. One of Google's ethical researchers was fired in 2021, in part because of a paper raising a number of concerns over the hidden costs of building ever larger LLMs.[25, 26]

Social and Societal Consequences of AI

If AI is primarily a matter of algorithms, then many of those algorithms have been commercially developed to maximize the economic benefits of so-called network effects. One dimension of the network effect is the way size increases linearly to a point where size *itself* becomes a source of further growth. This is one of the main reasons we find it easier to join Facebook or Amazon than to leave. A second dimension of the network effect is the development of what has been called 'the attention economy.' In this new socially-interconnected paradigm, the tools for AI have been harnessed for both economic and political purposes. In economic terms American social psychologist Shoshana Zuboff has done much to identify and then critique what she calls 'surveillance capitalism' by which the predictive powers of AI algorithms enable a behaviour-oriented futures market in which advertisers pay more or less depending on how likely the algorithm suggests we are to purchase their goods or services.[27] The benefit of an algorithm that is tuned to find underlying patterns and correlations to which I too might belong is that Spotify or YouTube or Amazon become very adept at recommending songs and videos and goods and services that I do indeed find pleasurable. The darker side, however, is that this process of tuning works in both directions. Those iterative algorithmic recommendations also tune *us* and *our* behaviour. This tuning of human being can, however counterintuitively, shrink an individual's access to the wider world by, for example, presenting the results of a web search using an opaque ranking system tuned to prioritize your propensity to click on a link rather than its value for information or even truth. There is now increasing empirical evidence for the way in which recommender algorithms seek to maximize our attention in order to profit from our time on a service by playing on specific psychological traits that enhance outrage, magnify discord and even incite some kinds of self-harm.[28]

The tools for AI have been harnessed for both economic and political purposes

The tools of AI have been used both to identify and to exploit certain psychological traits of human being which history may yet decide has preferentially benefited some politicians and a certain kind of politics to the broader harm of society as a whole.

On the other hand, AI is proving to be a fantastic tool for addressing some of the deepest challenges human beings face in the midst of an increasingly complex world, not least the twin threats of the climate and biosphere emergencies. From boosting efficiency in logistics and calibrating power distribution across complex networks in real time, to satellite navigation that redirects traffic to alleviate congestion, to identifying isolated endangered animals in vast tracts of jungle, to taking spoken words and instantly translating them into a foreign language. AI is contributing practically and visibly to both human flourishing and to monitoring our overexploitation of the natural habitat.

Governance: By Whom and For Whom?

AI can also be a tool of manipulation and for the economic and political instrumentalization of human being. How this happens differs from country to country across the world. In the Western world, surveillance is generally a mercantile endeavour using cookies and other tracking technologies, while in China the tools of AI are simultaneously available to both businesses and the state for the purposes of profit but also of social control and, in the case of ethnic minorities like the Uighur, of state oppression. Oppression of the socially marginalized need not be intentional for it to be problematic. Safiya Noble has exposed the way algorithms embedded in search engines reinforce racism by suggesting auto-fill options to complete the search phrase on the basis of similar word associations from other searches. Google changed their algorithm only after Noble had shown what happens when a user asks 'Why are black women so…?' The offensive options that Google's autocomplete algorithm suggested were drawn from biases it replicated from the underlying data.[29, 30]

One of the most pressing consequences of AI will be on the future of work

There is a well-known quotation among technology futurologists that 'The future is here, it's just not very evenly distributed.'[31] One of the most pressing but uneven consequences of AI will be on the future of work. The historical record offers some guidance here. Horses, not to mention those who cleared the city streets of their dung, were put out of jobs in their millions at the end of the nineteenth and beginning of the twentieth centuries. Lift operators made only a brief appearance in the early twentieth century until the role was successfully automated. And the job of airline pilot might conceivably last little more than a century in total. At its best, AI will be able to automate away some of the least-fulfilling and most dangerous jobs our present-day economy depends upon, like working in hazardous and contaminated environments or dull and repetitive tasks like sorting and packing. But there is some debate about whether this-AI powered fourth industrial revolution will be a net creator or net eliminator of jobs. So-called generative AI now threatens creative tasks like graphic design as well. Robot Process Automation (RPA) is already eradicating a wide variety of jobs in factories and logistics that underpin much of the modern economy. Micro-tasking sites like Amazon Mechanical Turk and CrowdFlower dehumanize work by atomizing individual jobs, isolating them from their final purpose and isolating the workers who complete them. The risk is that newly AI-mediated roles will further rob work of its inherent dignity.

In sum, then, the practical theological reality is that AI, like any other tool, can be used variously and for good or for ill. In which case questions of governance must remain connected to issues of human character and moral responsibility. We must be careful not to impoverish ourselves by outsourcing moral questions to narrow tools that have no ethical compass except whatever we try to program into them and therefore no ability independently to recognize or resist socially destructive biases embedded in the data we feed them.[32] A video recommender-algorithm, it must be remembered, 'sees' only numerical metrics relating to the viewer and the video-file it 'recommends,' not the violent or harrowing images to which any of those numbers may attach.

A Missional Response to AI

6

AI is unlikely to be the last tool we ever invent. In itself it offers neither an unmitigated good nor an irredeemable threat to human flourishing. In which case, the five Anglican Marks of Mission provide a helpful framework for a practical and missional response.

To Proclaim the Good News of the Kingdom

Our hope rests on God rather than our own effort or invention alone. Therefore, we should resist the more extreme rhetorical and utopian ambition around AI. In particular we should be ready both to recognize and reject an anthropology or natural theology that depends on a reductive view of human being and/or a metaphysically-elevated view of the outputs of mathematically-tuned algorithms as in some way fellow-citizens of the kingdom of God. The kingdom of God is our primary source of hope and purpose and all of our AI tools should be turned towards closing the gap between God's will in heaven and what is done on earth.

To Teach, Baptize and Nurture New Believers

The tools of AI are shaping *us* as well as our shaping of *them*. Our mission is to welcome, utilize and benefit from the good gifts of God, including those present in AI, while remembering their limitations. This will keep us vigilant for the ill effects that follow from creating tools made ever more convincingly in our own image. The perennial tradition of Christianity makes clear that making and being disciples is not a matter of propositional or intellectual knowledge alone. It is an intensely practical matter which concerns also the formation of a Christlike character. This will involve resisting the addictive and provocative design features that so many tools of AI intentionally target, not only for ourselves but for the vulnerable and especially for our children and younger generations. AI can be a wonderful aid for learning, but cultivating proper and proportionate use of smart and mobile devices in particular is a practical and missional task in its own right.

To Respond to Human Need by Loving Service

Similarly, there is a vast mission field that the network effects of companies like Twitter and Facebook now make accessible with ease. Small and isolated church communities can use digital technologies to connect with congregants across geographical time and space. But the mission field is full of thorns as well. Loving service using AI to respond to human need will include the esoteric, like using satellite geo-sensing data to coordinate flood response for isolated individuals in an expanse too vast to search by human eye.

But loving service also includes the tone we adopt on social media and the courage to speak up for the abused and marginalized. Which will, of course, involve noticing that they are there; the deliberately-cultivated charms of our algorithmically curated notifications and feeds, at least where they are designed to serve the economic interests of advertisers and businesses, can all too easily provide us with digital blinkers, saturating our attention and not merely encouraging us to avert our gaze from the poor and needy but causing us never even to be aware of their existence.

To Transform Unjust Structures of Society, to Challenge Violence of Every Kind and Pursue Peace and Reconciliation

AI is a way of looking at the world through human eyes because, without telling the algorithm what patterns to look for, we still have to tell it what a pattern is and how to begin to look for them. One urgent missional response to AI relates to the way that data contains embedded patterns of discrimination and injustice. Training images labelled with unconscious biases have led to algorithms associating black people with racist tropes, while predictive policing algorithms have used historical data to miscategorize black convicts as more likely to reoffend than white prisoners because, fundamentally, most offenders in the data were black. The tools of AI can be used to identify, causally account for, and even address these meta-patterns and their underlying biases, but they can also be used naively to propagate them. One missional response is to campaign for greater transparency of commercially-proprietary algorithms and better access for both academic researchers and civil society organisations to engage in ethical audit.

Furthermore, the deployment as well as the development of the tools AI must not ignore the *digital divide*. This divide is not only a matter of access or cost. It also comes through assumptions and demands of service providers for reading comprehension abilities and/or the practical understanding of how to use IT devices that society's most marginalized members simply cannot provide. Today, still only around half of the global population have access to the internet; of those, billions cannot access information or services in their own mother tongue.

To Strive to Safeguard the Integrity of Creation, and Sustain and Renew the Life of the Earth

Given the rapidly escalating threats to both climate and biosphere this fifth mark is an increasingly urgent and substantial dimension of mission. Proof of work blockchains are an unsustainable tool. Large language models are becoming extremely energy intensive to train while our appetite for AI and its data depends in turn on the mining and fabrication of physical resources for storage, access, and processing. The cloud is actually a vast physical network and the amount of data it contains is currently estimated to be doubling about every two years.[33] What data we choose to store, how and where we choose to store it and how frequently we dispose of our old devices in order to upgrade to the latest model are all matters that affect the integrity of creation in addition to how we use these AI-enabled smart tools from day to day.

7 Conclusion

AI is now a fundamental component of modern Western society, actively aiding human flourishing in a variety of ways.[34] But AI is not the golden ticket to an imagined future, whether wonderful or catastrophic. It is a dual-use tool with potential in either direction and the choice(s) belongs to *us*. Consequently, evaluation of how best to use and how further to develop this powerful and important new tool should include three carefully considered factors.

First, the enduring scientific and philosophical mysteries attending freedom and consciousness. We must be careful that the pragmatic setting aside of metaphysical mysteries does not lead to an impoverished view of human being becoming normalized. Rational inference and reason are important, and are marks of intelligence. But so are wisdom, empathy, the apprehension of the sublime and the moral and spiritual formation of character. Secondly, an adequate evaluation of AI must grasp the additional complications posed by language's remarkable and innate flexibility to shape meaning. Language is, itself, a multifunctional tool. Thirdly, we must continue to ponder what it means, fully, to be a *human* being. We are the final frame for deciding whether AI can fully replicate the whole gamut of human life or merely mimic some parts of it. Whatever else we say that AI can do today it emphatically cannot love, or rejoice, or sacrifice, or freely choose mercy instead of justice as we human beings can—and must.

Sensitivity to all three of these dimensions is essential for locating and keeping the debate(s) about AI in the right philosophical and theological register. Consequently, a fully Christian response to AI will want to engage with biblical anthropology, including both sin and eschatology.

Cumulatively that reflection will empower us to welcome potential while also recognizing hype, rejecting temptations to reduce and diminish the human, and motivating us to resist the identifiable harms as we seek mutual and collective flourishing.

Notes

1 https://www.bbc.co.uk/news/uk-65746524 (accessed 24 June 2023).

2 N Polson and J Scott, *AIQ* (London: Penguin, 2019) p 5.

3 https://www.technologyreview.com/2021/10/05/1036519/facebook-whistleblower-frances-haugen-algorithms/ (accessed 9 June 2023).

4 M Wooldridge, *A Brief History of Artificial Intelligence* (New York: Flatiron, 2021) p 17.

5 'Google engineer says LaMDA AI system may have its own feelings,' C Vallance, 13 June 2022, https://www.bbc.co.uk/news/technology-61784011 (accessed 10 June 2023). For the transcript itself see Blake Lemoine, 11 June 2022, 'Is LaMDA Sentient?—an Interview,' https://cajundiscordian.medium.com/is-lamda-sentient-an-interview-ea64d916d917 (accessed 10 June 2023).

6 A Turing, 1950, 'Computing Machinery and Intelligence,' *Mind*, Volume 59 (236) pp 433–460.

7 Imagine during a pandemic the detection of malignant melanomas can only be done by analysis of a photograph provided by the patient, and that the detection is much more reliable with those of one skin colour or tone rather than another. This presents a practical challenge, one which accusations of bias may serve unhelpfully to deflect.

8 J Searle, 1980, 'Minds, Brains and Programs,' *Behavioral and Brain Sciences*, 3: 417–57, available at searle.minds.brains.programs.bbs.1980.pdf (csulb.edu) (accessed 10 June 2023).

9 A 'LaMDA,' as a *language* model, cannot, for example, compose music or draw a stick figure. A single AI product, though, could well have a variety of capabilities under a single name; ChatGPT and GPT4 have both 'sat' (a term which certainly does seem to need scare quotes!) examinations involving both mathematics and essay writing. See https://writings.stephenwolfram.com/2023/03/chatgpt-gets-its-wolfram-superpowers/ for discussion of extending the capabilities of large language models (LLMs such as ChatGPT) with mathematical capacities (accessed 24 June 2023).

10 R Williams, *The Edge of Words* (London: Bloomsbury, 2014) p 117.

11 Y N Harari, *Homo Deus* (London: Vintage Books, 2017); see also N Thompson, (2018), 'How Humans Get Hacked: Yuval Noah Harari and Tristan Harris Talk with Wired,' https://www.wired.com/video/watch/yuval-harari-tristan-harris-humans-get-hacked (accessed 24 June 2023).

12 J M Soskice, *Metaphor and Religious Language* (Oxford: Clarendon Press, 1985).

13 https://www.computerworld.com/article/3039713/people-trusted-this-robot-in-an-emergency-even-when-it-led-them-astray.html (accessed 24 June 2023).

14 For a fuller description see https://en.wikipedia.org/wiki/ELIZA (accessed 24 June 2023).

15 P Harrison, *The Territories of Science and Religion* (Chicago: UCP, 2015) p 133.

16 R Kurzweil (1999), 'Ray Kurzweil on The Age of Spiritual Machines: A 1999 TV interview,' https://www.kurzweilai.net/ray-kurzweil-on-the-age-of-spiritual-machines-a-1999-tv-interview (accessed 24 June 2023).

17 See for example T Chivers, *The AI Does Not Hate You* (London: Orion, 2019).

18 Those who prefer a techno-utopian ending still mirror the modern scientistic conception of progress, this time with science and technology combining to open the route to self-salvation and immortality as (ironically, given the generally materialist predispositions of the worldview) disembodied information. See, for cogent critique of these views, M Midgley, *Science as Salvation* (London: Routledge, 1992).

19 https://www.catholic.org/encyclopedia/view.php?id=10963/ (accessed 24 June 2023).

20 P Natarajan, 'Alexa enters the "age of self": More-autonomous machine learning systems will make Alexa more self-aware, self-learning, and self-service,' https://www.amazon.science/blog/alexa-enters-the-age-of-self (accessed 24 June 2023).

21 On the distance still to run see M Wooldridge, *The Road to Conscious Machines* (London: Pelican, 2021) and E J Larson, *The Myth of Artificial Intelligence: Why Computers Can't Think the Way We Do* (Harvard: Belknap Press, 2021).

22 K Crawford, *Atlas of AI* (Yale: Yale University Press, 2021).

23 For an example in wildlife conservation see https://www.wildlabs.net/community-announcement/state-conservation-technology-2021 (accessed 24 June 2023).

24 https://ewastemonitor.info/ (accessed 24 June 2023).

25 T Gebru *et al*, 'On the Dangers of Stochastic Parrots: Can Language Models Be Too Big? 'https://dl.acm.org/doi/10.1145/3442188.3445922 (accessed 24 June 2023).

26 Some of our new technology tools are *designed* to be deliberately energy *in*efficient. Public blockchains, of which Bitcoin is the best known, while not themselves a type of AI have been designed using the principle of 'proof of work' (PoW) to deter attacks on the chain. The problem is that, by design, PoW blockchains do not become faster or more energy efficient as they expand in size. They merely consume more resources because the computational mining effort required also scales arbitrarily to keep the Bitcoin reward rate stable at one block appended every ten minutes or so.

27 S Zuboff, *Surveillance Capitalism* (New York: Profile, 2019).

28 K Tiffany, 'I Made the World's Blandest Facebook Profile, Just to See What Happens,' *The Atlantic*, 19 November 2021, https://www.theatlantic.com/technology/archive/2021/11/facebook-experiment-toxic-centrist-content/620731/ (accessed 10 June 2023).

29 S U Noble, *Algorithms of Oppression* (New York: New York University Press, 2018).

30 Plans are under discussion for regulatory and watchdog functions in relation to AI, with predictable competition for the prestige and perhaps the business of hosting such a body. H Zeffman and M Ledwith, 'Plans for British AI watchdog to keep tabs on global threats,' *The Times* (London) 3 June 2023, p 4.

31 The quotation is attributed to the sci-fi author William Gibson https://quoteinvestigator.com/2012/01/24/future-has-arrived/ (accessed 10 June 2023).

32 V Eubanks, *Automating Inequality* (New York: Picador, 2019).

33 Big Data Growth Statistics to Blow Your Mind (or, What is a Yottabyte Anyway?) https://www.aparavi.com/resources-blog/data-growth-statistics-blow-your-mind (accessed 10 June 2023).

34 https://beebom.com/examples-of-artificial-intelligence/ (accessed 10 June 2023).